Ireland

D0786115

An Ireland Travel Guide Written By An Irish.

The Best Travel Tips By a Local.

Table of Contents

About Our Guides - Why They Are Unique

We were travelers really tired of the typical boring travel guides. In most cases, wikipedia is much better, complete and dynamic. When we traveled, we tried to ask friends, or friends of friends who were "locals". That is where we got the best tips by far, the most valuable ones about our travel destinations.

This guide tries to do the same as the "ask a local", but it is (maybe!) better organized and more complete. In all our guides, we hire a "local" writer, and then we edit to be sure that the guide is complete, unique, fun and interesting. Typically we won't add too many maps or photos, since you can have all that on the internet and we like to give you only unique and original content that you won't find easily.

Since we use different writers for each city, you will see (after you fall in love with our guides and download more than one), that they are not standardized. Each city is different, each "local" is different, and each guide is different. And we really like that.

Thanks for being here and we really hope that you like it. Enjoy!

Chapter 1: Preface

So you're planning to visit Ireland? Excellent decision, my friend - you'll find us to be warm and friendly people who will make you feel truly welcome.

I don't like to boast, but we really have it all: Ireland combines a strong and vibrant culture stretching back thousands of years with vibrant cities featuring all the perks of modern life. We're a small nation and we like to keep our options open. And the good news is that because the entire island is less than 85 thousand square kilometers, you really can come here and see (and do!) everything.

Have you come to experience our dynamic and cosmopolitan cities? Or have you come to surf the world-famous Aileen's Wave? Are you hankering to go horseback riding through the surf or to spend a day at the races? Whatever activity makes your heart beat faster, you'll find something here to make you happy.

There are two important things you need to know about Ireland and the Irish. The first is that we're a proud and passionate race. When we commit to something we run with it all the way, whether it's a TV comedy about a trio of priests or a way of life that includes good food, good music and connection with the very soil of this island we live on. Don't worry, though; we're welcoming people and we'll be very happy to share our passions with you.

The second important thing is that we love to have fun, and if that comes with dressing up and - preferably - a parade, then we'll be so much happier. We have festivals and celebrations throughout the year, and during the summer you'll find at least one somewhere in the country every weekend. We celebrate everything from matchmaking to Halloween, and we don't do it in a small way.

Most of our festivals are laid back and homely, with a strong connection to the land and life as it has been here for us for hundreds of years. If you hanker for something more high-brow or sophisticated, we promise not to disappoint you. We're democratic people, and that means that we can find a celebration to suit any taste. Consider yourself challenged to ask, and we'll point you in the right direction.

Some practicalities: we use two currencies here in Ireland. The Republic of Ireland is part of the Eurozone, and so our currency is the euro. These are the same notes and coins used in all of the other countries of the Eurozone, and so you have no need for currency exchange when travelling between one and the other. This also allows you to directly compare prices, which can be very useful.

Northern Ireland is a part of the United Kingdom and uses the British Pound as its currency. The notes used here are specific to Northern Ireland and must be exchanged when moving to other countries within the British Isles. The pound tends to be worth slightly more than the euro, although the exact proportion can change.

Our banks and post offices all have a Bureau de Change, and you'll also find independent money-changers in all of our airports, cities and towns. We do have a very wide network of ATMs, and so long as your card has the MasterCard or Visa symbol, it's likely you can use any of them. Similarly, your credit or debit card will be accepted by the vast majority of venues.

Our electricity supply is 220V, and we use flat, 3-head plugs. If you need an adapter then they're easily purchased in any electrical shop or even more easily, at the airport. Our public phones tend to accept cards rather than coins, and the code to dial out is 00 followed by your country code. We use a different terminology of bed sizes too. What in the United States is called a Queen is in Ireland a King size, so don't be disappointed if that's what you book and you find it smaller than you expected.

Although we're situated in the northern part of the continent, our weather tends to be temperate with only the occasional exception. This is because of the Gulf Stream, which bathes our western coast in warm waters from Florida and points further south. Thanks to this (and we are very grateful), our winter temperatures average around 8°C and our summer around 20°C.

Our sunniest months are May and June and you'll find better weather in the Southeast of the country than in the North West. This would be lovely if it didn't rain so much - between 150 and 220 days a year on average, which you'll agree is a little overabundant. The plus side is that it keeps our grass green.

Our official languages are both Irish and English, but practically you'll find that all official, social and financial business is conducted in English. Most of us can string a sentence or two together in Irish, some considerably more than that, but expressing ourselves in English is no hardship and is in fact preferable for practically all of us.

If you have any pressing questions that aren't answered here then don't feel shy about asking a local. We are really happy to help; we're not just putting it on for the tourists. I'm confident that a local contact can answer your question, whatever it is. And if he can't then he'll most definitely know somebody who can.

Figure 1 Ireland by Trent Strohm, courtesy of Flickr

Chapter 2: Getting Around

Although we're a small country with a limited area, you'll still need to think about how you intend to get from place to place once you're here. And, of course, the first step is to actually arrive. Being an island, the ways of doing that are limited but uncomplicated. Put simply: you either arrive by plane or you come by boat.

After that, you need to figure out how to get around. Would you prefer to rent a car and set your own schedule or is the comfort (and WiFi!) of a train journey more to your taste? Do you have a set and rigid itinerary or are you free to fall in with the available bus and train times? Would you like to join a tour, or do you prefer to remain independent? These are all considerations to think about before you decide how you plan to travel.

Your next choice is whether you wish to travel for fun instead of with the intention of getting to a set destination. Do you enjoy bike riding or galloping through the waves on horseback? Have you always hankered to rent a barge and float along the river? Or is your preference to recapture the charm of yesteryear and rent a horse and trap to carry you in style? We can offer all of this and more.

Figure 2 Inis Mor, Aran by David McSpadden, courtesy of Flickr

Chapter 3: Arriving In Ireland

The first question is: how do you get here?

As you know (don't you?), Ireland is an island on the western edge of Europe. We're quite close to England, Wales, Scotland and France, and reachable by air from any country in the world in a matter of hours. Simply put, coming by air really is your simplest option. Experiencing the world at the slight remove of an ocean surrounding us allows us to really develop our national identity, which we think is a good thing.

As it happens, the first non-stop transatlantic flight touched down in Galway in June of 1919, and we've been welcoming visitors by air ever since. And if you believe Irish legend, we're the ones who first discovered North America by currach and about a thousand years before Christopher Columbus got around the continent. You see, we really do like to get out there and do things; we're also very fond of a good story.

Ireland has five principal airports: one each in Dublin, Knock and Shannon, and two in Belfast. This means that the first thing you'll see of our country is one of its cities; believe me, they're well worth experiencing and will repay your time. But don't worry if it's really our famous green you want, though; we're a small country and even in the centre of Dublin, the countryside isn't far away. If you're planning on staying at one of the hotels nearby, odds are it has a complimentary shuttle service to take you door to door. If your first trip will take you slightly further afield, don't worry. All of our airports are well served by regular bus services and once you get to the city centre, the entire country is open to you. Or if you don't feel quite that independent just yet, you can always take a cab.

Your first task will be to pass through immigration and customs but don't worry: there are very seldom delays, and the officials are both friendly and helpful. We want you to enjoy your visit and we make that clear as soon as you step onto our soil. It is best to check out any visa requirements before you leave home, though; it's much easier to take care of any essentials from there rather than facing the possibility of being turned back before you even get through the airport.

Although legend tells that some hardy souls braved the crossing to the USA in hide-and-wicker currachs, unless you're Brendan the Navigator it's not something we recommend. Being an island, we are boat friendly: ferries and hovercraft from Scotland, Wales, England and France arrive all along our eastern seaboard. It's a fantastic way to travel in good weather but unfortunately, that isn't something we can promise you.

Our primary ports of arrival are Ringaskiddy in County Cork, Dun Laoghaire in County Dublin, Rosslare in County Wexford and Belfast and Larne in County Antrim, Northern Ireland. That's a pretty reasonable spread, so it might be a good idea to think about your onward journey before you decide which one suits best. Because ferries all arrive from countries within the European Union, immigration control is less stringent than at airports. If you aren't paying attention you may not see it at all.

Another choice, and one that isn't common these days, is to come by coach. Of course, being an island, that will mean travelling by ferry anyway, but at least the logistics and organization are headaches for the coach company and not you. All you need to do is climb on board, choose your seat and wait to get off on the other end. Through Eurolines, the European coach network, you can come here from destinations as far-flung as Moscow or Helsinki without having to leave your seat. Coaches come in to Busaras, the main bus station in Dublin, and from there you can either settle into the capital or find a convenient way to travel further.

No matter how you get here, the important thing is that you've arrived and you're ready to make yourself at home.

Figure 3 Aer Lingus Boeing 757-200 (EI-LBR) by Canadian Pacific, courtesy of Flickr

Chapter 4: Getting From Place To Place

We're a small country but even so, we have nothing to be ashamed of in the way of infrastructure. By some international standards you may find our less frequented roads narrow and bumpy, but an increasing area is served by city to city motorway, making travel simple and straightforward. Our transport system may not be perfect but it's modern, reliable, and we'll get you to where we promised we would. You'll always have options, and it isn't too difficult to figure out which will be best for you.

Your first option is to rent a car. We're pretty responsible road users here and, as long as you make yourself aware of the rules of the road before you get behind the wheel, then you'll be just as safe as you would be at home. The airports all have a selection of rental companies for you to choose from, including several Irish-owned ones.

You also have the option of renting a camper van from Celtic Campervans; with this option you have a way to get around and somewhere to stay all in one. There are campsites with utilities in most towns and if you don't want to choose that route, then you can just pull up in a quiet corner overnight.

We drive on the left side of the road here and our distances are measured in kilometers (although the older people will still give them to you in miles). A decade back, our driving habits were pretty cavalier: we didn't worry too much about driving licenses or about maintaining our vehicles. A series of government clampdowns changed that and nowadays you can expect the people and cars you encounter on the road to meet reasonable standards of safety.

Ireland has a reasonable selection of motorways, making city to city travel a simple matter. The M1 links Dublin to Belfast - for example - and similar roads will take you to Cork, Galway, Limerick, Navan and Sligo. Take care though: some of our motorways - the M3 for example - are tolled, so be sure to have some Euros on you.

If you don't care to drive yourself, there are still a lot of options available for getting around. We have a pretty decent train network when travelling to and from the capital, Dublin; although other towns and cities aren't very well linked to each other. The trains are regular and comfortable and while you're travelling, you'll have the opportunity to either buy drinks, snacks and sandwiches in-seat or to take advantage of the full menu that the buffet car offers.

As well as print newspapers available to buy on board, all of our trains offer complementary WiFi and also power ports for charging phones and laptops, which helps time to pass while you're travelling. And you can bring your pet with you too.

Irish Rail also offers a service called Tours by Rail, which provides a tour of the country from the comfort of a scheduled train. They offer day tours and longer trips - up to nine days - with a planned itinerary and overnight accommodation provided. If you're free to fit your schedule to one of the tours offered, then this is an excellent way to see our country in style. And of course, you can link several shorter tours together in whatever pattern serves you best.

Irish Rail also looks after the Dart service. DART stands for Dublin Area Rapid Transport and that's exactly what it is: a speedy way to get around Dublin City. It runs from Howth in the north to Greystones in County Wicklow and not only does it allow you to conveniently move from place to place, but it also offers spectacular views of the coast and the best scenery Dublin has to offer. For your stay in the capital the DART is definitely a transport option to consider.

Trains are an excellent way to get around but by their nature they're limited in the places they can take you. If your planned route doesn't lend itself to travel by rail and you don't care to rent a car and drive yourself, you can always take a bus. Buses do go, literally, everywhere. There isn't a town, village or wide spot in the road that isn't served by a regular bus service. All of our cities and towns have a bus station and you'll see stops by the side of the road in the most unlikely places. Service is regular but the disadvantage is that only the bus stations have the timetables on display.

If you're planning to leave from a smaller place, you need to either look the timetable up online or ask a friendly local for the information. Fortunately, you'll find any number of locals available and happy to help. Bus Éireann also offers an Open Road fare for those who plan to do a lot of travelling.

Because we're a small country, we don't plan on doing a lot of travelling by air - everything we need is close enough to reach in a few hours' driving. When we do want to fly, however, it depends on where you want to go. Dublin is linked to all of the international and regional airports but unfortunately aren't linked to each other. To get from Belfast to Cork for example, the most time-effective way is to travel through London. If you're in the capital and want to fly, there are options that will take you to any part of the country. The one exception to this is Aer Arann, the carrier that serves the Aran Islands off the coast of Galway. Granted they only serve that one route but it's an easy and cost-effective way to visit the islands and a trip well worth taking. They offer several flights daily to and from each of the three islands and also offer sight-seeing flights along the shoreline if an island visit isn't to your tastes.

Figure 4 Train approaching Balbriggan station by William Murphy, courtesy of Flickr

Chapter 5: Getting Out and about

We're a small country but even so, we have nothing to be ashamed of in the way of infrastructure. By some international standards you may find our less frequented roads narrow and bumpy, but an increasing area is served by city to city motors.

So you've arrived in the country and found your way to an area that suits you - well done! Now the hard work is done and the only travel you need to do is for fun. Ireland's dependence on vehicles isn't much more than a decade old and you can still find plenty of fun things to do that will also get you around to see the sights.

Horse Riding

Ireland has a long and rich history with horses. When the rest of the world moved on to cars and motorized vehicles we held true to our four-legged companions. Yes, these days pretty much all of us drive to get where we need to go, but we still love our horses. In fact, Ireland is often called "The Land of the Horse" and the animals take a central role in many of our myths and legends.

On Oisín's return from Tir na nÓg, for example, the Queen of the Fae warns Oisín not to descend from the back of his magical horse or he would die. An accident leads him to ignore her words and he gains 100 years in an instant and turns into a dying old man.

If you love them as much as we do, you can take a horse riding holiday where you immerse yourself completely in the horse riding life. You can stay in one of the equestrian centers dotted all over the country, take instruction from the friendly and qualified trainers to improve your skill level and spend your days cantering through the sand dunes or galloping cross-country.

If you're travelling with somebody who isn't as horse-mad as you are, some of our centers offer combination holidays in partnership with golf courses or cookery schools, or even with English language schools. And with your evenings free to spend however you want, a horse riding holiday can offer the best of all worlds.

If you love your horses but not enough to make them the focus of your entire holiday, you can always take a one-day activity ride or put together a combination of different activities to suit your itinerary. Make sure you choose a centre that's A.I.R.E. (Association of Irish Riding Establishments) recognized and you'll have a safe ride supervised by a qualified instructor. Depending on where you visit, you can trek in the mountains, gallop through the waves on a beach ride or practice jumping either in the ring or as part of a cross-country trek. You'll meet interesting people, spend the day doing what you love and see the country exactly the way our ancestors did - from the back of a horse.

Figure 5 Into the Sea by Nicola Corboy, courtesy of Flickr

Bicycle

Our roads may seem narrow and bumpy to those accustomed to autobahns and interstates, but they're absolutely perfect for cycling. As a nation we've taken the activity with passion and you'll see cyclists, both amateur and professional, using bicycles to get to where they're going, as you travel from place to place.

Our varied countryside offers many activities for trail biking, cross-country and biking into the mountains, and you can choose from guided tours with a knowledgeable guide and fascinating planned stopping points; or if you're more independent, simple bicycle rental and the chance to plan your own route.

As with horseback riding, many centers offer holidays specifically focused around the bicycle. As with any tour of the island, you'll travel from place to place but the advantage is that not only your bicycle but your accommodation is provided as part of the package, which means that your luggage is transferred from place to place and you won't need to worry about carting bags and cases along with you while you cycle.

You can combine lessons on equipment maintenance with guided tours through some of the most gorgeous areas of the country. If you choose a guided tour then your guide will have insider knowledge of the best of our coffee shops and restaurants too, and so you're guaranteed an enjoyable stop when you need to recharge your batteries. Unguided tours are also an option, combining the advantage of luggage transfer and planned accommodation with the opportunity to travel at your own pace or to take side trips if you wish to.

If you'd prefer a longer trip you could consider the 6 days 3 coasts tour which runs out of Dungarvan in Waterford. The itinerary includes the coasts of counties Wexford, Waterford and Cork. As well as allowing you to see the spectacular views up close and personal, stops include a traditional glass-blowing workshop, a 12th Century round tower, Hook Lighthouse with its spectacular vantage point over the Atlantic Ocean.

Bike rental is available pretty much everywhere and if all you really want is a suitable and well-maintained bicycle to allow you to do your own thing, then you won't have any trouble finding one. Our road users are familiar with and respectful of cyclists, and we have close to a thousand dedicated trails with varying levels of difficulty for those who want to get off the grid for a while.

Horse and trap

You want to get out of the car and really see the country but the strenuous activity of a biking tour just isn't for you? In that case, how about renting a horse-drawn caravan? A light wooden covered wagon that can accommodate up to four people and offers space to prepare meals and to sleep while still being light enough for a single horse to pull. The nomadic Travelling gypsies of Ireland have travelled in exactly this way for hundreds of years.

You don't need any great knowledge of horses to consider this option, your rental operator will instruct you on how to take care of your horse and you'll most certainly know a lot more when your trip is over. Most operators will also offer suggestions about local events and areas you might like to visit and there could be no better way to see the country and meet the people. You'll most definitely have a talking point!

If caring for a horse and guiding your own caravan sounds too daunting to make for a relaxing holiday then don't worry, you have other choices. You can take a jaunting car with an experienced driver to tour some of our most beautiful and spectacular places, including Kenmare Castle and the Lakes of Killarney in Kerry.

One of our best-regarded trips is a full-day tour through the Gap of Dunloe in the Macgillycuddy Reeks Mountains of Kerry. The scenery is spectacular and the pace is leisurely, you'll feel as you've been transported back in time to the days when a horse and trap was the only way to travel.

Another option is the horse and trap tour of Inis Mór, the largest of the Aran Islands off County Galway's coastline. Not only will your experienced guide show you the ancient architecture of the island, but you can also see the celebrated seal colonies and the spectacular Dun Aonghasa fort - a prehistoric structure guarding our westernmost shore from the perils that might come from the ocean.

You don't need to be in the countryside to travel by horse and carriage: you can tour our cities this way too. Carriages are convertible to guard against bad weather and come with lamps and blankets for an authentic experience, especially when touring the Georgian areas of Dublin. A perfect way for an authentic, guided trip, that's conducted in luxury.

Figure 6 O'Connell Street, Dublin by Maureen Robinson, courtesy of Flickr

Make use of our waterways

Want to do something a bit more exciting and energetic with your time? Ever thought about whitewater tubing? The idea is that you're strapped into a large tube (the type used at water parks) and pushed into the Inny River to enjoy running its rapids. It sounds terrifying - to me at least - but it's actually perfectly safe and can be enjoyed by children as young as eight. Once you get the hang of it, you can even play a game of river polo as you float along.

Don't forget, you'll also be warm and dry inside a wetsuit, a must in our Irish climate, even in the summer. If the idea sparks your interest, then look for the Outdoor Discovery Adventure Company in Ballymahon, County Longford, it's one of the few places here that you can give it a try.

You might be thinking that whitewater tubing sounds like fun but you'd prefer to be more in charge of your trip downriver. In that case, have you thought about kayaking? There are a range of trips available, starting with a leisurely kayak across Lough Lein in Killarney. It's a full-day trip with an experienced guide, and not only will you get to explore small wooded islands and deep limestone caves; you'll also get to visit an ancient leper colony. Not as exciting as it sounds; the only inhabitants these days are the red deer.

Or if river kayaking is more your style, you have plenty to choose from. I recommend Go with the Flow River Adventures in County Kilkenny for a range from simple to more challenging river ranges.

Your kayaking choices don't end there; you can always think about sea kayaking. Available all along the western coast, you can choose a sea view of Galway City for a completely different perspective. Or you could take a sunset trip into Dingle Bay in County Kerry to visit with Fungi the dolphin and watch the sun go down over the Atlantic Ocean.

If all of that sounds much too energetic and dangerous for you, don't feel discouraged. If the idea of a water centered activity appeals to you but you don't care to put yourself at the river's mercy in a kayak, you might consider renting a barge and travelling in style. The only suitable river is the River Shannon, which runs almost the full length of the country to the west, but you get to choose between a self-navigated narrow-boat and a small hotel type with a captain and a chef.

Boat trips by sea

Ireland has long been considered one of the world's best sea angling destinations. This shouldn't come as a surprise: we have over three thousand kilometers of coast and fishermen here have earned their living fishing for generations. The boats tend to come with a crew in situ and they'll accept about twelve guests or fewer.

Thanks to the Gulf Stream and the natural variety of our shoreline, sea life here is extremely varied with over eighty species of fish swimming around. If you're lucky, you can catch a record-breaking cod, a 400kg tuna or even a conger eel. Equipment and local knowledge come as standard, all you need to bring is your enthusiasm.

It's a sociable way to pass an afternoon and at least your audience will be inclined to believe you when you tell them about the one that got away.

It isn't all about fishing, of course. Boat trips out to sea are an excellent way to explore not only our wild and savage coast but the bird and animal life that make their home here. From Dublin you can take a tour close to Ireland's Eye, a bird sanctuary just off shore of the capital where you can see breeding colonies of gannets, cormorants and even puffins.

The island also boasts a ruined 19th Century Martello tower as well as several fine rock-climbing courses, although naturally climbing is forbidden during the birds' breeding season. You can also visit the Rockabill Lighthouse, a fascinating building built and 1855 and still operating, though it has been automated since 1989.

A boat trip I recommend as not to be missed is the eco marine tour into Dingle Bay in County Kerry. This tour specializes in watching whales and dolphins, with bottlenose dolphins, porpoises and Minka whales commonly seen. Killer whales and humpback whales also make appearances sometimes, if you take the trip in the late summer or autumn and you'll also frequently come almost within touching distance of a basking shark.

Note the "almost" there, please!

You'll also see thousands of nesting seabirds, hundreds of grey seals and even red deer on the islands. The Marine Tours people are passionate about sustainable eco tourism, and they combine their chartered trips with a census taking to log the marine life spotted in the bay on a daily basis. With a local wildlife expert on board to answer any questions you might have, this is a boat trip not to be missed.

Figure 7 by Anthony Furlong, courtesy of Flickr

Chapter 6: Where To Go – Cities

We've talked about how to get to Ireland and about how to get around once you arrive here. The next big question is where you should go and what to see once you get there.

We're a country of two halves: the cutting edge sophistication of our cities is a strong contrast to the slow pace and traditional lifestyle of the rest of the country. As a nation of artists and dreamers, we've found a way to live with the duality, with most of our people partaking of both as the need and circumstance suggests. The distances are small here after all, and it's easy to spend an afternoon drowsing by a river bank followed by a night sampling all of the delights a modern city has to offer. The sheep farmer you exchange nods with may plan an evening at the National Concert Hall, and the cab driver might spend his evenings and weekends in a small cottage with a fairy fort in the garden.

Both halves are rich in culture and artistic excellence, although it might be expressed differently in each.

Dublin, for example, abounds with newly penned plays and modern takes on old classics, while deep in the countryside the bank manager rubs shoulders with the milkman in a production of an Irish favorite.

Neither lifestyle is right or wrong, nor does a wise man seek balance between the two. To understand us properly, you should try to spend time in both environments and bring together the best of both.

Our cities are limited in number and each has its own character, so that no matter which order you visit them in, you always feel like you're coming to somewhere new.

Dublin

I've often heard it said that when visiting Dublin the first place to visit should be Kilmainham Gaol. It may strike you as odd that a place so steeped in suffering and misery should be so pivotal in understanding Ireland and the Irish. Although the gaol housed many criminals and unsavory types over its long history, it is enshrined in the Irish psyche as the place where so many of the martyrs of the 1916 rebellion were imprisoned and subsequently shot.

Here Joseph Plunkett married fiancée Grace Gifford mere hours before his execution, and James Connolly was shot to death while tied in a chair. Here within these damp and gloomy walls, you can feel the spark that ignited to make us a country.

Our capital has a lot to offer in terms of culture and heritage and one of the foremost is our Natural History Museum, known to generations of children here as the Dead Zoo. It first opened in the 1850's and popular belief has it that it hasn't changed much since then. Certainly it still has a Victorian feel, with an Irish Room celebrating local flora and fauna, two more levels dedicated to the creatures of the rest of the world and some uncelebrated oddities such as the Kamikaze Eels under the hanging skeleton of an enormous whale. Located centrally in Merrion Street - and with free admission - the Dead Zoo repays a wet afternoon spent exploring all of its secret treasures.

Malahide Castle is a living piece of Ireland's history. Built by the Talbot family in the 12th century, it was home to the family until the 1970s when it passed into the possession of the state. You can take a tour of the castle, much of it exactly as it was when the Talbot family was in residence, spend time acquainting yourself with their colorful history in the Visitor Centre and, with luck, catch a glimpse of one of its resident ghosts.

You can also enjoy the walled Botanical Gardens with their celebration of horticultural excellence and, when you're ready to embrace the 21st century again, Malahide village is only a ten minute stroll away.

If you're visiting our capital and have the slightest interest in the arts, then the Abbey Theatre must form a central plank of your trip to Dublin. The theatre was founded in by a collective of Irish literary minds that included Sean O'Casey, John Millington Synge and W.B. Yeats. It was the first English-speaking theatre in the world to be funded by the state and, although the original building burned down in 1955, the tradition of the theatre has continued unquenched.

If you choose to enjoy a play in the Abbey, you can expect only the highest standards of this Irish performance art.

Figure 8 Galway City, Ireland by Douglas Pfeiffer Cardoso, courtesy of Flickr

Cork

When us Irish think of Cork, we think first of Blarney Castle and the world-celebrated Blarney Stone. Legend has it that a person who kisses the stone will receive the gift of "being able to deceive without offending", or silver-tongued eloquence.

The origins of the stone itself are murky. Stories variously describe it as the pillow of Saint Columba on the island of Iona, an oracular tool brought to Ireland by Jeremiah, the stone from which Moses caused water to pour or the Scottish Stone of Destiny, stolen from the Irish and later restored in gratitude for some battle or other. Its true power is believed to have been revealed by a witch saved from drowning and it has offered its benediction to all comers from that day onwards.

It's no easy matter to receive that blessing. Located high above the ground in Blarney Castle, the stone offers its powers only to those who can bend over backwards into a mighty drop to reach it where it hangs. Kissing it is much more easily done nowadays, with iron railings to hold on to and a careful assistant to supervise, but still not for the faint of heart or for those who are afraid of heights.

Cork's English Market is acknowledged as Ireland's most prestigious covered food market, and it's worth a visit should you find yourself anywhere nearby. Trading here goes on as it has since 1788, with prime quality natural foodstuffs - some traditional and others new to Ireland and the people of Cork - are bought and sold with gusto and good humor. Named the English Market to differentiate it from a nearby Irish Market, please don't think that it's a type of 18th century chain supermarket. Cork's English Market is as Irish as they come.

Another location well worth visiting in Cork is the Crawford Art Gallery, housed in the stunning old Custom House. Admission is free and the gallery celebrates the work of artists from the surrounding areas of Munster, with over 2,000 permanent exhibitions ranging from 18th century portraiture to cutting edge modern video installations.

Although the collection was begun in 1819, its current curators haven't been lax in maintaining and updating its offerings, either historic or new. The permanent exhibitions are always worth taking time over, especially the sculpture, and they frequently have spectacular temporary fixtures such as Picasso, and the casts of Greek and Roman sculptures that gave the Gallery its beginning.

Galway

Galway is both a stunning, ancient city that retains its medieval streets and stone-clad buildings and also a booming party town beloved of students throughout the country. Add to that the fact that it's a traditional seaside location for generations of families and you'll find that the buzz of people having fun invigorates you as soon as you set foot onto its cobbles.

The city is known locally as the City of the Tribes, named for the 14 merchant families who dominated its commerce and governance from the 13th to the 19th Centuries. The name "The Tribes of Galway" was given to them as a derogatory label by Oliver Cromwell in his suppression of Ireland, but they adopted it happily and wore it as a badge of pride.

Galway has a small city centre and is a city that is best seen on foot. Walking tours run dail, and with knowledgeable local guides, you will begin at the park at the centre of Eyre Square and the city, explore Lynch's Castle which is the oldest building in Ireland still used commercially, learn the history of the iconic Spanish Arch and see part of the walls built in the 12th century and still an integral part of the city. Don't be surprised to find many local people on the tour with you; we Irish love our history and are happy to immerse ourselves in it.

Also well worth a visit is the Claddagh Museum in Quay Street. The Claddagh ring is a well-known symbol of love and marriage in Ireland, used as a wedding ring in the area for over four hundred years. Its distinctive design of two hands holding a heart which bears a crown is represented by the motto "Let Love and Friendship Reign".

The museum explores both the history of the ring and the fascinating story of the goldsmith who designed it, Richard Joyce, who was captured by pirates on the way to the West Indies and sold as a slave to a

Moorish goldsmith who taught him the trade. Although focused primarily on the history of the Claddagh ring, the museum also features famine memorabilia, prehistoric stone axe-heads and photographs of the city throughout the ages. Entry is free of charge and a visit is strongly recommended.

Another place well worth visiting in Galway is the Aquarium. You'll find it on the promenade in Salthill and the first thing you'll experience when you walk through the doors is the splash tank and its one hundred tones of splashing salt water. It's designed to mimic the ecosystem of our West coast, and in it you'll find Sea Bass who are as at home here as they would be in the real crashing waves.

From an interactive ray tank where the rays often stick their heads above the surface of the water, to see what's going on to the glass-sided deep ocean exhibitions where you'll see deep-water fish such as cod and small sharks, the environments here are as close to natural as the aquarium people can make them.

Exhibitions include freshwater and harbor and even a wrecks exhibit where you can understand how the shipwrecks that dot our shore have become home to the denizens of the deep. Visit the aquarium and you'll come out with a newfound love and respect for the sea.

Figure 9 Galway City, Ireland by Douglas Pfeiffer Cardoso, courtesy of Flickr

Limerick

Limerick is Ireland's fourth city, and is often overlooked by locals and tourists alike. The central part of the city is known as King's Island, and is formed by a distributary of the River Shannon. Writings by Ptolemy show that the site was already occupied in 150AD and has continued uninterrupted as a population centre although it has long since outgrown the bounds of the island.

When in Limerick, the Jim Kemmy museum is very well worth a visit. It celebrates the history of the city in all its diverse forms, from rent books and postcards of last century's dwellers to a sword presented to the city by Queen Elizabeth I to a meteorite, the largest ever to fall in either Ireland or Britain, which was recovered from the nearby town of Adare. One of the featured exhibitions celebrates Limerick Lace, a form of fine lacing unique to the city that was in high demand in the 19th Century and which brought much industry to the city.

If you plan to spend time in the city, I strongly recommend a trip to the Lough Gur Heritage Centre.

The centre's design is inspired by the Neolithic dwellings unearthed locally and its aim is to explore six thousand years of the area's known history. Here you'll learn about the first farmers in the area, their implements, lifestyles and burial practices. The centre focuses not just on history but on custom, folklore and storytelling and its focus is a joyful rather than an academic retelling of the story of the area.

Chapter 6: Where To Go – Countryside

Of course, Ireland isn't all about its cities. In our centers of population you'll find an exploration of who we are as a people, from ancient and modern history to the arts and our place in the world. All of this is fascinating and informs who we are as a nation and a people; we place immense value on having it available.

In the countryside, rather than explore who we are we simply live it. If you wish to share with us the entertainments that we look forward to in our weekends and evenings, you have to be ready to simply have fun. Don't worry, we'll help you get started.

Ailwee Cave Complex

The Ailwee Cave is located in the centre of the Burren, a karst landscape and an area of stark natural beauty. The cave complex runs underneath, unsuspected by those who haven't visited it previously. Its story is an interesting one; discovered in the 1940s by a farmer who followed his dog into its mouth, he didn't share his knowledge of the cave system for almost thirty years. When he did finally let cavers in on his secret, the response was instant and enthusiastic and their initial exploration quickly resulted in a push to open the cave complex to everyone.

The system runs for over a kilometer and leads to the heart of the mountain; dated at over 350 thousand years old it is considerably older than any of the other caves in the region. Its features include an underground river and spectacular waterfall, the bones of extinct bears, spectacular configurations of stalagmites and stalactites and bridged chasms of spine-chilling depth. Not all of the tunnels are open to the public, but enough of them are to make for an ethereal and otherworldly experience.

Cliffs of Moher

Located not far from the cave complex, the Cliffs of Moher are a series of sea cliffs along Ireland's border with the Atlantic Ocean, standing at 214 meters at their highest point. They run for eight kilometers along the shore and on a clear day, they allow views of the Aran Islands, Connemara to the north and Dingle peninsula to the south. A visitor here can't fail to be reminded of how small we are in the face of the immensity of nature.

The cliffs can be appreciated by either a boat trip along their base, or a walk along their tops - don't worry, the path is perfectly safe and the area is protected by a barrier of ropes to prevent foolhardy individuals from coming too close to the sheer drop.

You can take a guided tour or enjoy the walk at your own pace and a series of Cliff Buskers along the route play traditional Irish music to help you enjoy the atmosphere. A visitor centre is available to provide any advice or information you may need, particularly about the wide variety of seabirds and raptors that nest in the area.

The sheer drop and the sound of Atlantic waves breaking at the cliff base is both soothing and invigorating, and a visit to the location is always enjoyed by visitors and returning locals alike.

*Figure 12 Small Tortoiseshell by Bart Busschots,
courtesy of Flickr*

Surfing

When you think about surfing your mind might automatically lead you to Hawaii, California or Australia, but in fact the west coast of Ireland boasts some of the finest waves in the world and our children learn to be comfortable on a board from a young age. The eternal drawback of course, is our climate; but with a well-fitting wetsuit and a judicious choice of day and time there's no better place on earth than the crest of a wave.

If you're a surfer or move in those circles then you'll have heard of Aileen's Wave. It's a giant wave formed by just the right weather conditions and the geological structure of the Cliffs of Moher that has been identified as the earth's closest thing to a perfect wave. The wave itself can soar to over 12 meters and you should bear in mind that only highly experienced surfers should consider riding it.

For the rest of us, one of the best surf locations is Bundoran, in County Donegal. It's home to several excellent surf schools and is conveniently close to several excellent surfing beaches, including Tullan Strand. Because of the Strand's formation, it often has waves when other sites are completely flat and its waves are suitable for everybody from beginner to old hand.

For the more experienced surfer, The Peak is only a few miles further along the shore and offers one of the best reef breaks in the country. Time to get your wetsuit on and get into the water.

Straffan Butterfly Farm

For a complete change of pace, you should consider the Straffan Butterfly Farm in Straffan, County Kildare, which has been open since 1986. The attraction combines the delicate beauty of the country's butterflies with a strong drive towards awareness and conservation, all centred on the mini jungle of the Tropical House, where the butterflies fly and breed freely.

You can see their entire life cycle take place around you from eggs to caterpillars to chrysalis and, if you're lucky, you'll see an adult butterfly climb out of its chrysalis and test its wings for the first time. If you're a photographer, then the Tropical House almost guarantees some spectacular shots.

In the Exhibition Centre you can see butterflies from all over the world and learn all that you ever wanted to know about their life cycles and living conditions. Here also you will see other creatures from tarantulas to scorpions living quietly on display. If framed butterflies are to your liking you can take home a framed example of a fritillary or a Painted Lady. The farm takes pains to point out that these are surplus examples of butterflies bred on site and have not been collected from the wild.

The Butterfly Farm has long been a local favorite for families and schools to visit, and many children have grown up to bring their own young ones to enjoy the serenity of the Tropical House jungle.

Visit an open farm

As our farmers struggle to maintain their livelihoods in the current difficult economic climate, many have learned to use the fascination of non-farmers to their advantage. Open farms are springing up throughout the country and most offer an excellent combination of education and entertainment.

The Castle Adventure Farm, for example, is located just outside Ireland's oldest settlement of Ballyshannon in County Donegal. The farm not only allows visitors to familiarize themselves with cattle, sheep and pigs, but orphaned lambs can be bottle fed, a JCB digger is available for driving lessons and there's even an emu. All of this represents an ordinary working day for thousands of farmers throughout the country (except for the emu!) but as our employment increasingly pulls us away from the old ways of the agricultural life, we hanker after it and pay money to those who can allow us to share it for a time.

Regardless of where in the country you stay you will find an open farm within a short travelling distance, I recommend visiting if you wish to see how regular farm life is lived, even if it is on display.

Eagles Flying

If immersing yourself in nature is your ideal way of spending an afternoon, you should consider exploring the Eagles Flying Centre in County Sligo. The centre is officially a raptor research centre and is home to over

75 species of animals and birds of prey as diverse as owls, eagles and vultures. At its inception in 1999, the centre was intended for research purposes only but overwhelming local interest soon pushed them to open their doors to visitors.

Flying demonstrations take place twice a day and you'll be captivated by the swoosh of owl feathers over your head, vultures perching by your bench or if you're very lucky, the feeling of golden eagle talons clamping onto your arm. The exhibition isn't for everybody and if you have a bird phobia you would be well advised to stick to cuddling the raccoons and hedgehogs in the indoor area. If you've always yearned to be close to a regal bird of prey however, a visit to Eagles Flying is something you'll never forget.

Fota Wildlife Park

Ireland has only one wildlife park named Fota Park, situated on Fota Island and only at a twenty minute drive from Cork City. The park has been opened since the 1980's and has been a location of bemused Irish interest ever since. Everybody loves the zoo, but lurking at the back of our minds is the knowledge that the animals really aren't happy in such close captivity. Fota Wildlife Park resolves that worry in a big way.

The park has carefully planned walkways and a train around the perimeter and there's enough to see and do to provide a full day of entertainment. From cheetahs to rhinos and bisons, there's always something new to see. If your interests don't lie with animals, you can always relax in the 27 acres of gardens attached to the park. Because the park is a self-financing charity development is continuously ongoing and currently plans are afoot to develop an Asian jungle area.

And for a small oasis of peace at the centre of all this family fun, the coffee shop is located right beside the children's play park so that you can enjoy a few moments of adult conversation while the little ones play right under your eye.

Bunratty Castle

If you're at all interested in Ireland's medieval history then a visit to Bunratty Castle in County Clare - close to Limerick City - is a must. The castle was built in the 15th Century on the site of a ruined Viking trading camp and is filled with authentic medieval furnishings and paintings for a thoroughly genuine feel. Unlike many period buildings, the castle isn't experienced by guided tour; the entire area is free for you to explore and you'll be met in many areas by experienced people who will answer any questions you may have.

Attached to the castle is a folk village, a reconstruction of how ordinary Irish people might have lived in the 19th Century. Here you can smell bread baking, visit the school or the doctor's home and see Ireland as it would authentically have been two centuries ago. A plus is that the bar and restaurant serves real food and beverages and you can take a moment to relax surrounded by the area's history.

Bunratty Castle banquets have been held on the site in modern times for over fifty years, but unlike many other medieval banquet experiences this one is held in a place where people truly made merry in exactly this fashion. When you arrive, you will be greeted by a piper and a "bite of friendship" will mark you as a guest, and therefore you'll be protected by the rules of hospitality from any harm during your stay.

Authentic food and mead are offered first to the Lord in the appropriate manner before being served to the guests and music, drama and pageantry are provided along with the meal. The Bunratty Banquet is a unique and immersive experience that should be enjoyed at least once.

Rock of Cashel

The rock of Cashel is a spectacular group of medieval buildings, including a round tower and a high cross, located in the quiet town of Cashel in County Tipperary. Most of the buildings in the complex date from the 12th and 13th century, although the architecture is a mix that includes features from earlier and later times.

In the area folktale tells that the rock originally formed part of the Devil's Bit Mountain, 30 kilometers to the north. When St. Patrick banished the devil from the mountain, the rock flew high into the air and came down in its present location. In more historic terms the Rock of Cashel was the traditional seat of the kings of Munster.

Furthermore, legend has it that it was here that King Aonghus, King of Munster, was converted to Christianity by St. Patrick, patron saint and first missionary to Ireland, in the 5th Century. At that time Cashel rivaled Tara as a centre of power in Ireland and King Aonghus' acceptance of the new faith of Christianity did much to cement its legitimacy in the region.

This is one site where the guided tour is much preferable to figuring it out by yourself. There are so many layers of architecture and construction at the site, not to mention myth and legend, that only a knowledgeable guide can allow you to appreciate it properly.

Figure 13 Rock of Cashel by Irish Typepad, courtesy of Flickr

Craggaunowen Heritage Centre

Craggaunowen open air museum is also a historical site you'll find in County Clare but unlike Bunratty Castle, it explores a much earlier period of history. The main exhibition centers on a reconstructed crannog, a man-made island that the Mesolithic people built within our lakes. On the crannog you can explore several mud and wattle round houses built, as they would have been in early medieval times along with a tower overlooking the entrance and the traditional outdoor cooking site used in those days.

Another fascinating item housed here is the boat Tim Severin, used to recreate St. Brendan's supposed voyage to the Americas in the 6th century. Tim built the boat in the traditional way using oak, ash, ox hides, leather thongs and wool grease. Tim sailed the boat to the Hebrides, Iceland and ultimately Greenland in an exultant justification of the Brendan story as history rather than legend. As every Irish person will tell you, it was an Irishman rather than Christopher Columbus who truly discovered America.

Ireland's most haunted house

If you find yourself in the area of County Wexford and have a strong constitution, you might consider visiting Loftus Hall. The Hall is considered to be Ireland's most haunted building and is said to be troubled not only by the ghost of a disturbed young woman from the 18th Century, but by the spirit of the devil himself. It is said that the devil's departure through the roof left a hole that could never be repaired and that successive exorcisms by Protestant ministers and Catholic priests have been unable to rid the house of its tarnish.

If you should wish to experience Loftus Hall's spectral ambience for yourself, you can enroll on one of the daytime tours that explore the house's interior and delve into its murky history. Night time tours are also available, though not for the faint hearted. You can challenge yourself to take part in an overnight Lockdown tour with a licensed paranormal investigator, where you fully immerse yourself in the atmosphere of the house. After this tour a debriefing session is considered necessary before you are permitted to go on your way.

This tour is considered to be very good fun and the site has been investigated in a serious manner by several international paranormal experts. Maybe you'll be the next person to encounter one of the ghosts here.

Tin Soldier Factory

As a complete change of pace and to cleanse your psyche from the unsettling tour of Loftus House, why not consider visiting the Prince August toy soldier factory in Macroom in County Cork? This little known factory is the primary manufacturer of tin soldiers and their moulds in the world and the only one in Europe and, if you wish to call in, they'll be delighted to let you watch them work. 95% of their items are sold online, so don't expect a large showroom, but the display area features both an enormous representation of the Battle of Waterloo and a reproduction of Sam and Frodo's confrontation with the giant spider, Shelob.

The great thing about the Prince August factory is that not only can you watch the figures being made but for children big and small you can also choose your mould and take part yourself. After a brief demonstration visitors cast their own figure and then paint it to their own specifications, creating a fantastic keepsake to remember that day. For a daytrip like no other, suitable in any weather, be warned that the Prince August factory might spark a life-long interest in miniatures.

Northern Ireland

Northern Ireland has its share both of the cultural peaks of the cities and the relaxed fun of the countryside. As it is officially a different country with distinct governance and a separate currency, it is best to consider it as a whole and separate from the rest of the Island.

This doesn't by any means suggest that the people and places of Northern Ireland are different or in any way less Irish, but the logistical difficulties of enjoying what it has to offer are a consideration when planning a day trip or a short visit.

Although the troubles are no longer a feature of everyday life and security measures have relaxed a great deal, as with any new place, it might be wise to be aware of your surroundings. Certain times of the year such as the 12th July, or 7th December in Derry are more likely to see friction than others and it is wise to consider this when making travel plans.

Figure 14 Giant's Causeway by Chris Lofqvist, courtesy of Flickr

Belfast

The primary city of Northern Ireland is Belfast. It's a vibrant and rapidly growing city, home to a prestigious university and several colleges that bring young people onto its streets. The Queen's University forms the centre of the city's University Quarter and is at the end of the so-called Golden Mile of pubs and restaurants. It is one of the youngest and most vibrant and a must visit area for those new to the city.

Running parallel to the Golden Mile is Botanic Avenue, home to cafés, charity shops and second hand bookshops and predominantly occupied by students and young people. This area is known as the Holy lands of Belfast due to the habit of naming its streets after areas in the East - Damascus Street, Jerusalem Street, Palestine Street and many others. The area is predominantly used as short term accommodation by students, which makes it a fun place to visit but not one that lends itself to long-term residents.

Belfast is internationally known as the place where the Titanic was built and it celebrates this history in the form of the Titanic Centre, a dedicated visitor centre devoted to the history and ultimate destruction of the doomed vessel. It also commits to the ship's current location, exploring the ocean where she rests and the sea life that might make its home around her.

Dedicated galleries explore subjects from the Belfast environment in which the ship came to be to its actual construction and launch and to the experience of its sinking and the myths and legends that have sprung up in its wake. A truly immersive experience. If you have even the slightest interest in the Titanic or its maiden voyage, then the Titanic Centre will inform and entertain you for as long as you wish.

Belfast centers around its City Hall, a distinctive Edwardian building of Portland stone that shows well in the daylight and even better when illuminated at night. Free tours of the building run Monday to Saturday and explore its structure and history as a symbol of the fact that Belfast is a relatively new city, receiving town status only in the 17th Century and becoming a city only at the end of the 19th Century. Belfast's people are justifiably proud of its rapid journey to success.

If you are interested in history and politics of Northern Ireland, then you should definitely consider a trip to visit the Stormont Parliament Buildings. Free tours run twice a day from Monday to Friday and you will need to undergo a security check before the tour begins.

You will have the opportunity to watch assembly members debate if they are in session.

Stormont Building's use to house the Northern Ireland is relatively recent; prior to 1998 this area of Ireland was directly governed by London. 1998 was the year that the main parties in Northern Ireland reached the Good Friday Agreement (Easter tends to be a dynamic time here!) that led to power sharing and home rule.

If politics isn't your inclination, then you may enjoy a trip to the W5 science and discovery centre in the city's Cathedral Quarter. W5 represents the five questions "Who? What? Where? When? Why?" and symbolizes the spirit of fun and adventure to be found in the centre.

The entrance atrium is currently filled by an interactive sculpture titled Climbit - you've guessed it, the sculpture resembles a combination maze, jungle gym and climbing wall and invites passersby to use it to take to the skies. The atrium is also home to RoboThespian, an interactive actor and performer whose purpose is to inform and entertain.

No review could do justice to exhibits as diverse as hygiene, cartoon animation and wind turbine design to name but a few; my advice is to visit and see for yourself. This centre really is among the best our nation has to offer and if you intend to visit only one exhibition during your time in Ireland, I'd vote for this one.

Figure 15 Derry's Walls by horslips5, courtesy of Flickr

Derry City

Northern Ireland's second city - named variously as Derry, Londonderry or the Maiden City - is considerably older than Belfast, tracing its beginnings back to the year 546. The fact that even the city's name is in dispute would imply that the city is a site of conflict, but in fact it's a friendly place and trouble is uncommon here. When it does flare it's usually the result of too much merry-making in one of the city's fine pubs.

The city centre is completely enclosed in walls constructed in the 17th Century, and the fact that these walls have never been breached gives it the nickname The Maiden City. Derry is, in fact, the only completely walled city in either Ireland or the British Isles.

Although the city has long since expanded past these walls, their top is a broad and tree-lined walkway allowing a pleasant view of the city centre as a whole, and makes for an interesting afternoon walk if weather allows. If you'd prefer to be guided then walking tours follow the route regularly and always have a wealth of information and stories about the city and its people.

Build into the walls at Bishop Gate, near the courthouse, you will find the Verbal Arts Centre -

Ireland's only centre dedicated to literature and the language arts. Within its walls you'll find a graphic arts festival, storytelling events, a poetry festival and even a crime novel festival to celebrate the ethos of Halloween. If your passion is words then you'll find something to please you within these walls.

The first Saturday in December features a celebration in the city known as "the closing of the gates" or Lundy Day. It commemorates an incident from 7th December 1688 when the city was besieged by King James' armies. The city's leadership, headed by Robert Lundy, had reached a secret agreement with James' forces to surrender at the first opportunity but as the armies approached, a number of apprentice boys in the city ran to close the city's gates against the invaders.

The apprentice boys' bravery is commemorated in an annual parade, beginning with cannon fire at midnight, featuring a parade through the city's streets in the afternoon and culminating in a bonfire at which an effigy of Lundy is hung and burnt (the original gentleman suffered no such fate). The celebration is an interesting experience for those in Derry at the time, although it should be noted that the majority of the city's people do not endorse this view of events and tensions can sometimes ensue.

In 2013 Derry was the first British city to be recognized as a City of Culture, and the city has chosen to interpret the concept broadly, with events as diverse as celebrations of dance and jazz to workshops in cinematic sound and urban design. I may be biased, but I truly believe that if you're looking for culture Derry has everything you might possibly want.

Ulster American Folk Park

The people in Northern Ireland may belong to a spur of the United Kingdom, but in their history and experiences they are truly Irish. Nowhere is this more obvious than in the Ulster American Folk Park, an open-air museum and reconstruction of village life in Ireland in the 18th century.

The park is staffed by volunteers, who go about daily business as it would have been lived at that time and who offer visitors demonstrations of the various skills such as spinning, printing, cooking and various other necessary tasks. The area is split between Old World, or Ireland at that time and New World, or the America in which the emigrants fought for a better life. Joining the two is a Ship and Dockside area representing the long and sometimes dangerous passage between the two.

The park is ideally suited to host special events, two of which are the Making Connections festival - which features poetry and traditional Irish music and dance, and the Bluegrass festival which focuses more on the music found in the emigrants' destination. This park is uplifting because it has the right idea -- instead of bemoaning difficult times in our history let's celebrate them. They did, after all, make us the people we are today.

Game of Thrones tours

Speaking of the people we are today, did you know that the HBO award-winning show Game of Thrones is principally recorded in Northern Ireland?

Several tours are available to take you to the primary sites, with some even offering the same transportation that the cast and crew use to get from place to place. Many of the important locations are found in Strangford, including Castle Ward which is used represented in the show as Winterfell.

Costumes are available for rental and you can take an archery lesson in the exact spot where Bran was taught by Jon Snow. Travel a short distance to Tollymore Forest Park where the white walkers first encroached on the lands of men and where the Stark family first encountered a dying direwolf and her pups, unwittingly beginning their unwilling slide into adventure.

You won't meet any of the cast or crew on these tours, but that may be for the best. Standing alone in places that have experienced these great battles and desperate acts it's easier to imagine that you're a part of their story.

Giant's Causeway

If tours of the countryside are what interest you, you should consider a visit to the world-famous Giant's Causeway in County Antrim, on Ireland's northernmost coast. The story I learned as a child is that the causeway got its name from the giant Finn McCool, who created it in a fit of temper by grabbing handfuls of Antrim's rocky coast and hurling them into the sea. The rocks he threw fell in the form of a causeway, allowing him to confront a Scottish giant with whom he was in dispute (bad idea - go find the entire legend!).

The more prosaic version of the story is that the jigsaw-like formation of almost perfectly hexagonal columns - forty thousand of them - was formed by a flow of lava released by a volcanic eruption, each successive wave hardening as it reached the sea. Now that doesn't sound at all likely, does it?

Regardless of which version of the story you believe, the Causeway is a World Heritage site and will take your breath away. It can be reached directly by road or, the approach I would recommend, by means of a

Figure 16 Carrick-a-Rede Rope Bridge, Ballintoy by Fabio Casadei, courtesy of Flickr

Rathlin Island

While you're in the mood for tours, you should think about visiting Rathlin Island. It's the only inhabited island off Northern Ireland's coast and is located six miles to the north east. It's easily reached by a ferry that runs up to ten times a day from Ballycastle in the summer and to a more limited extent in the winter.

Its population is currently 125, a number that has been rising steadily in recent years and, because of its location, it has stronger ties to Scotland than any other part of Ireland, giving it a unique feeling in terms of culture. Its primary draw is its rugged scenery and spectacular ocean views, including the Antrim coast, Donegal and on a clear day even Scotland.

In practical terms, Rathlin has no bank and only limited ATM services. Few of the local businesses accept debit or credit cards meaning it is wise to plan ahead and bring cash. In reality, however, apart from food and drink there are limited opportunities to spend on the island. Visitors come mainly for the walking tours and to visit the seabird centre, which operates free of charge.

The island is a living example of an older style of life maintained today, not as a form of heritage or for the benefit of visitors but as a valid lifestyle choice.

Tour of the Bushmills Distillery

Ireland is famous for many things worldwide, and one of the foremost amongst them is our whiskey. It may surprise you to learn that Bushmills, one of our smoothest and most popular brands, is produced not in the Republic but in the civilized environs of Bushmills, County Down.

The Bushmills crowd is a very restrained lot, to the extent that they don't even allow access to their website unless the surfer provides a date of birth to prove that he or she is over eighteen and so of a legal age to be exposed to alcohol. We won't hold it against them, though; they've been distilling whiskey for a long time (over four hundred years - they're the oldest working distillery in Ireland) and they take their responsibilities seriously.

The tour begins in the mash house, where pure local water is combined with malted barley to make wort. This wort then has yeast added and the combination is triple distilled in the still house.

Bushmills focus on making small batches to very high standards, and this is reflected in the care they take in the barreling process. You can see the fully matured whiskies being barreled and, having worked up a thirst in the process, visit the gift shop to choose from a full selection of Bushmills products, some of which are only available on site.

When you taste the finish product, you'll be glad that they're so particular with what they do.

Armagh Planetarium

If you want to try something very different, you might consider a trip to the planetarium. Located in historic Armagh City, it's a centre for increasing public knowledge on astronomical matters, and it does this primarily by inviting visitors to view the amazing items in the cosmos.

The most interesting display is the Astropark, a scale model of the universe as we know it. Visitors can walk through our solar system or the Milky Way and come to understand in concrete terms how the stars and planets relate to one another. Models include the Hubble telescope, the International Space Station and other space-going vessels and satellites.

The Mars Room is also worth the time to visit, plus you can touch the 4.6 billion year old meteorite which happens to be the largest one on display in Ireland. As a way of locating oneself as a tiny part of a huge universe, the planetarium can't be beaten.

Chapter 7: Nightlife

One thing we Irish can do is party. Whether it's a national achievement or the third sunny day in a row, you'll find us to be a nation ready and eager to celebrate it. You'll be glad to hear that there are many options for you to join us in doing exactly that.

A few concrete details about Irish pubs: first, smoking is banned indoors but most bars offer a nominally outdoors smoking area that in reality is an extension of the craic inside. Second, the legal age at which a person can be served alcohol is eighteen and yes, the bar staff will ask for identification if they have any doubts. Third, closing time is 11:30pm Sunday to Thursday and 12:30am on the other days of the week. If a pub's been granted a late license, though, they'll serve until 2am.

The best part of the pub life apart from the music and the excellent Irish stout, is the conversation. We're gregarious people and if you're in our company we'll want to meet you and learn all about you. And be warned: being in our company means being within hailing distance.

Figure 17 Dublin! By Juan Salmoral, courtesy of Flickr

Ha'penny Bridge, Dublin

TUESDAY

7

FEBRUARY

S	M	T	W	T	F	S
			1	2	3	4
5	6	7	8	9	10	11
12	13	14	15	16	17	18
19	20	21	22	23	24	25
26	27	28				

Cities

Dublin's our capital and a city a large population of young people, so it makes sense that it's the place we go when we really want to let our hair down. The city's party area is called the Temple Bar and although tourists do naturally graduate there, you'll find that the majority of people having fun are locals. The Temple Bar is where you'll find good food and some of the country's oldest and most famous pubs. Prices can be higher here than in other parts of the city, but not universally, and it isn't hard to find somewhere that's more reasonably priced.

Even though Temple Bar concentrates the bars and restaurants into a dedicated area, it's far from the only place to go in the city. From the mega-club The Wright Venue in Swords to Lillies Bordello, where you might rub shoulders with a celebrity or two, the city has something for every taste. You might want to try the Bankers Comedy Club on Trinity Street for some of the country's best improv and stand-up. After all, there's nothing that makes an Irish person laugh more than talk of a banker.

But of course Dublin isn't our only option. For young, vibrant culture there's no place like Galway. It's a city with a small town feel - cobbled streets, a tiny city centre and the friendly feel unique to college towns. This means that the night spots are clustered within a small area - many of them are on Quay Street - and so if you don't like the mood or the music in your first choice, you can easily find someplace else more suited to your tastes. In the good weather the party spills onto the streets, so you can gauge the feel of a place without even walking through its doors. Wherever else you choose to visit during your time in Ireland, I strongly suggest you include Galway in your itinerary.

And then, of course, there's Belfast. It has a different feel to Galway or Dublin, more complex and grown-up, but that doesn't mean the people there don't know how to let their hair down and have fun. The Kremlin for example, is the largest gay club on the island and the Eglinton and the Botanic Inn cater for a mixed crowd of students and early twenties. And then there's Kelly's Cellars, an old time pub right in the city centre. If you want impromptu traditional music from the punters rather than a scheduled band, this is the place for you.

Countryside

Of course most of our living takes place outside of the cities. Our celebrations and commiserations, lazy summer evenings and short winter afternoons take place in the seaside towns and midland villages that the other parts of our life do, and it works very well for us.

One of the best things about small town night-life is that it's eclectic. A village pub is for everyone and a night out might mean a long, well-lubricated conversation with a sixty-year-old truck driver on one side and an eighteen-year-old theology student on the other. It may seem counter-intuitive but the smaller the population base the more likely we are to spend time with people outside of our limited range of age and experience. And that can only make life richer for all of us.

Our cities are vibrant hubs of international commerce and commingling, but it's the ceol agus caint (music and conversation) that we steep ourselves in every Sunday afternoon and on random Tuesday nights that makes us the people we are.

Chapter 8: Events

You've probably figured this out already, but we Irish love our parties. Every town in the country has found something to celebrate, from the Sea Sessions Surf and Music Festival in Bundoran, County Donegal to the Matchmaking Festival in Lisdoonvarna, County Clare, and if you wanted to you could find a street party every weekend of the summer.

Mainly we celebrate music, food and the arts, but you can find anything from ploughing championships to the celebration of the fictional Irish priest Father Ted. Truthfully, here in Ireland you can find a party to match any one of your interests. I've made a list of some of the biggest ones for you below.

Figure 18 Fireworks over Derry by Greg Clarke, courtesy of Flickr

Tedfest - Aran Islands, County Galway, February

Father Ted is a cult Irish TV comedy show about priests (trust me, it's much funnier than it sounds) and because the show was set on the fictional Craggy Island, the festival takes place on the very real Aran Mór Island off the coast of County Galway. For a complete immersion into the tongue-in-cheek perspective from which we Irish see ourselves, there's nothing that comes remotely close to the revelry of competitions, costumes and quotations. Prepare to be either invigorated by Mrs. Doyle's frequently offered cups of tea or baffled by the cow that may be either small or far away. If you're a Father Ted aficionado you need to book early, as tickets are limited by the size of the island and are snapped up quickly. In the words of the great priest himself, "Careful now!"

Figure 19 St. Patrick's Day, Dublin by LenDog64, courtesy of Flickr

St. Patrick's Day -- Nationwide, March

We Irish are proud of our culture, which is why our day of national celebration has been carried all over the world with our emigrating population. No matter where you're from, no doubt you've seen it celebrated in a parade, or a bunch of shamrock, or even just green-colored lemonade. And even though New York's parade is usually bigger, there's nowhere in the world an Irishman wants to spend 17th March except our capital city of Dublin. But don't be concerned about those of us who, for whatever reason, can't be there; every town and village has its own parade, thoughtfully timed so that we have time to get to as many as we choose to enjoy. After all, why stop at a single party?

Bloomsday - Dublin, June

We don't just love a party, we're a nation of poets and visionaries and even those of us who don't know our sonnet from our iambic pentameter are proud of those of us who have risen above the common stock. And from this comes that great celebration of James Joyce,

Bloomsday. Bloomsday is held on 16th June every year, the date on which the events in Ulysses, Joyce's greatest work, took place (its main character is named Leopold Bloom, hence the festival's name) and the city is filled with men and women in Edwardian costume, retracing the route that Bloom takes in the book and reading key passages in the pubs and open air. Even if you're not a literature aficionado, it's an atmosphere not to be missed.

Sea Sessions - Bundoran, County Donegal, June

It's a little-known fact that on the west coast of Ireland we love to surf. The fact that Irish people love music is more widely known but although we love our traditional fiddles and bodhráns, we haven't allowed the modern music world to pass us by. We bring both of these facts together in Sea Sessions, a festival of surf and music held every June in Bundoran, County Donegal. This festival takes international performers like Example and Black Grape and adds to them the sheer unselfconscious fun of beach tag rugby and a sandcastle building competition. And of course, there's the surfing contest. This is one to get to if you want to see how we let our hair down on the west coast.

Cliff Diving Competition - Inis Mór, Aran Islands, June

The cliff diving championships are held on Inis Mór, the largest of the Aran Islands, and are a sight to behold. Brave or foolhardy individuals pit their luck against nature in diving from a high cliff into a natural pool known locally as the Serpent's Pit. The drop has been measured at 27 meters, or three times that of an Olympic diving competition.

Last year the island welcomed over three thousand spectators to the event, as well as 14 competitors from 9 different countries. The spectacle was breathtaking, with the sleepy island stirred up by the bravura of the competition and the sheer number of spectators alike.

Whether you intend to visit as a spectator or you're one of the brave and hardy contestants, aficionados will be treated to a genuine, if bemused, welcome.

Earagail Arts Festival - County Donegal, July

I know we talked about the Irish love of the arts when we discussed Bloomsday, but the Earagail Arts Festival is a quite different beast altogether. On Bloomsday, we celebrate an artist held up for the approval of the world, but in the Earagail Arts Festival we quite simply enjoy that spark of creativity in each of us.

It's bilingual, it's for the people and by the people, and it has everything from plays to circus performances to old-time storytellers. The whole idea of the festival is to take what people want to do, what people want to see, and do it. If you're looking for the real creativity of the real Irish people then here it is.

Fleadh Cheoil na hÉireann - Sligo, August

The name translates as The Music Festival of Ireland and that's exactly what it is. Officially, the Fleadh Cheoil is the premier competition for amateur musicians. It's a tradition stretching back thousands of years and today's Fleadh has everything, from professional musicians to impromptu sessions to classes for everybody, including absolute beginners.

All of our traditional instruments - bodhráns, uilleann pipes, fiddle and tin whistle, not to mention the purity of the human voice - come together to make something that's new every time. You've got music in the bars, music in the streets and music in everybody's hearts. If you're looking for Ireland's soul, then this is where you'll find it.

Ould Lammas Fair - Ballycastle, County Antrim, August

Tied to the ancient harvest celebrations of Lughnasadh, the Ould Lammas Fair has been held in Ballycastle on the last Monday and Tuesday of August since the seventeenth century. This is the festival of rural Ireland, celebrating farming life with stalls selling Yellowman (traditional honeycomb toffee) and farming equipment, face painting and horse-trading. This is how life in Ireland has been lived for hundreds of years, and thousands of us enjoy celebrating that.

If you choose to come to Ballycastle on fair day, leave your sophistication at the door and prepare to have some uncomplicated fun.

Galway Oyster Festival - Galway, September

We're an island nation who loves good food, and both of these facts come together in the Galway Oyster Festival held in Galway City, held each September to celebrate the opening of oyster season. It isn't just about oysters, though - as well as the oyster opening competition we also have a seafood trail where you can learn more about other types of seafood, cooking demonstrations, a Mardi Gras event and of course, some live music to help it go down easy. And a parade: Irish do love our parades.

Matchmaking Festival - Lisdoonvarna, County Clare, September

The Lisdoonvarna Matchmaking Festival is something us Irish are proud of but, at the same time, don't talk about much beyond our own shores. It's been running for over a hundred and fifty years and had its beginnings in the days when we were a rural nation and farmers didn't move much off their own plot of land.

Dances begin at 12 noon every day and run until the wee small hours, with set dancing displays and traditional music in the bars to set the tone and help people to relax.

Today, although some still visit in the hopes that the matchmaker will find them a spouse, most of the thousands of singles who flock to the town are looking for some fun. Don't expect this to be a sophisticated event - the focus is on making opportunities and, above all, simple enjoyment.

National Ploughing Championships - Ratheniska, County Laois, September

Although our cities do offer the cultural intricacies of a prime European location, many of us earn our living from the land. The National Ploughing Championships celebrates that by attracting over a quarter of a million visitors over its three-day event

Although the ploughing competition itself is the pinnacle of events held throughout the counties, there are also sheepdog trials, demonstrations of various farming equipment and prizes for cattle and sheep and pigs. And because we're Irish, you'll also hear music throughout the event.

The National Ploughing Championships remind us of our national identity and that we're proud of our agricultural heritage. They also remind us that all but a very few of us are no more than a generation or two separated from the land.

Halloween - Derry City, October

Did you know that the holiday of Halloween originated in Ireland? Not in its current form of course, but we have always celebrated Samhain, the death of summer on the last day of October. Derry City takes that tradition and gives it a modern spin, turning the day into a city-wide carnival of fun and the largest Halloween celebration in Europe. From the haunted house and night-time market - and yes, a parade - to the Horror Film Festival and Gothic Fancy Dress Ball, you'll find fun and chills enough to pique any interest. Derry doesn't ignore the children, but it doesn't forget either, that the origins of Samhain are decidedly grown up.

The festival concludes in a breathtaking fireworks show, made all the better by the fact that the people of the city come out in fancy dress to enjoy the spectacle. If you should find yourself unexpectedly free for the scary season, I strongly urge you to give Derry a visit.

Chapter 9: Sports

The people of Ireland work hard and we also play hard. You can see this in our music and our love of parades, but also in our sport. You'll find soccer matches on the big screen in pubs the length of the country, yes, but what we're really passionate about are our local games.

Hurling

You may think that the great game of hurling bears a strong resemblance to the British sport of hockey. You might think that, but you'd be dead wrong. Hurling came to Ireland with the Celtic people at the end of the last ice age and is older than our recorded history. It dates back over three thousand years and is the world's fastest field sport. One of our greatest legendary heroes, Cúchulainn, earned his name through quick thinking and his skill at the game. And don't think that the men have all the fun; the women's version is called camogie and shows exactly the same warrior spirit.

Put simply, the idea is to use a bent stick (camán) to hit the ball (sliotar) through the other team's goals. And of course, to prevent the opposing team from doing the same. There are more rules, but for basic enjoyment of the game that's all you need to know. We start our kids with tiny camáns (and helmets!) in nursery clubs and by the time they're old enough for the under-sevens teams, they've already developed basic skills and a hunger for the win.

The good news is that no matter where you go in Ireland, you'll see hurling played. If you want to experience truly skilled competition though, you'll need to visit the south of the country. Kilkenny, Tipperary and Cork are the acknowledged masters of the game and if you have the opportunity to attend a league or championship game in any of those counties, then you'll understand what we mean about passion. If you have the great good fortune to get to a Championship Final game, you'll be a hurling convert to the end of your days.

Figure 20 Killyon vrs Longwood - Meath Senior Hurling Championship by Peter Mooney, courtesy of Flickr

Gaelic Football

Our national football game bears no resemblance to soccer or American football and only a passing similarity to Australian Rules football. Unlike rugby the ball is round and slightly smaller than a soccer ball; the goalposts are similar to those in rugby and the ball may be handled under a strict set of rules. Gaelic doesn't fire our blood the way hurling does, but on the other hand it's played more often on grass fields and in school playgrounds, with no coach or referee smoothing play.

Because of this, more counties have a decent shot at progressing through the national Sam Maguire Cup competition held every summer. And having a stake means we take our county's performance very seriously. If you visit in the summer and you're wondering why every home and even car has a flag outside, now you know why.

It's all friendly competition, though. We pride ourselves on making sport a family event and even the most hotly contested match is family friendly, with no segregation of the spectators. You might find yourself sitting on a chilly stone bench alongside your bitterest rival, exchanging ham and cheese sandwiches and friendly banter. The conflict on the pitch is expected to stay there and any bad behavior in the crowd is viewed very unfavorably by the GAA and fans alike.

Gaelic football is more easily exported than hurling too, and many countries in the world have their own teams. In fact, the game is so inclusive that both London and New York's teams are considered to be honorary nationals and are included in the Sam Maguire Cup as honorary teams from Connacht (the smallest province).

Either team has ever come close to winning but then that isn't the point. You'll know if a county you're visiting has won the championship by the fact that the place will practically shut down the day after the win, with schools and workplaces closing to allow as many people as possible to welcome the victorious team home. Come if you can - it's always a great party.

Horse racing

It's a well-known fact that we Irish love our horses. You'll find their liquid eyes watching you from fields throughout the nation, and even in some built-up urban areas you may come across a pony grazing on a grass verge or a square of greenery. We're not content just to look at them, though; we want to see how fast they go.

Ireland's studs and trainers are a force to be reckoned with in international racing circles, and if your interests lie in that direction then a visit to the National Stud is an absolute must. Not only can you tour the stud and visit the incomparable horse museum, but if you have little ones they can be treated to a pony ride. Now that's something not to be missed.

Did you know that the steeplechase is an Irish invention? That's right, the first ever cross-country race from one steeple to another took place in Cork in the eighteenth century and we haven't stopped racing since. It's a much different affair nowadays and just because the beast is the same one traded at the Ould Lammas Fair doesn't mean that the mood of the occasion will be the same. A day at the races is an excuse to buy a new suit or dress and above all a new hat!

Not all Irish racing is accompanied by the formality of the Sunday best. A sport you won't hear about outside the country is sulky racing where light, two-wheeled carts are raced along the country's main roads, often by boys in their early teens. Needless to say the events aren't well regulated and are unlikely to be advertised in advance, but if you should chance upon one they're a good example of the Irish face we don't often show the world.

Chapter 10: History And Culture

As you will have realized having come so far through this guide, we are very proud of who we are and where we come from. We celebrate this by embracing our history and cultural identity, both by keeping our historic sites alive and by celebrating the music, the storytelling and the dance that have been passed down by our grandfathers and their grandfathers.

One area where we're conscious that we've failed is in our national language. Irish is taught in schools, studied from the age of four to the age of eighteen, and then promptly forgotten once the school gates shut behind us for the last time. There are odd enclaves where it persists as a first language, but these areas are shrinking and even there the locals can express themselves impeccably in English.

Efforts by officials and concerned groups continue and are making some headway, but for now our national language is a matter of national and notional pride rather than a real and living tongue.

Figure 21 The old days are gone! by Rick Wedzinga, courtesy of Flickr

The people of Ireland

It may seem to the casual visitor that Irish people form a homogenous whole with our fair skins, blue eyes and red hair, but in reality that's far from the case.

The first to come to Ireland were the Mesolithic people, who first arrived at what we now call Mountsandel in County Derry, almost ten thousand years ago. These people are remembered in our stories and legends as Fomorians, and cutting edge research suggests that they may have been short, with black hair and blue eyes just like many Irish people do today.

These people specialized in tombs; court tombs, passage tombs and dolmens, the mark they left on the land is still visible in sites such as Creevykeel in Sligo and Glantane East in County Clare.

Next came the Celts. They arrived in two waves, the first directly from Europe via France and Spain and the second through Britain and across from Scotland. It was these, tall and fair-skinned with light-colored hair, who gave us our Irish language and our stories of warrior chieftains and great acts of bravery.

The Celts were followed by the Vikings. They began raiding late in the 8th century, and over the next three hundred years they experienced greater or lesser success, building an overwinter settlement in Dublin and being pushed out of it again. They brought with them blond hair and blue eyes, a rare combination in Ireland today, and left a high number of their warriors buried in full battle regalia under the streets of Dublin.

Next to come were the Normans. They moved from France to Britain and consolidated there first before crossing the Irish Sea to settle in Ireland. They are responsible for the majority of our medieval castles and strongholds, and were stocky, medium to dark haired and fair skinned. Their major contribution to modern Ireland is the English language they brought with them.

A small but significant influence comes from the soldiers and sailors of the Spanish Armada who shipwrecked along our western coast. Most were murdered by the local people as they came to shore (not our finest hour as a nation), but some survived to settle and intermarry with the natives. They have given us our occasional short, brown-eyed and very dark individuals and the wealth of ships dotting the sea-beds off the coast of Sligo, Mayo and Galway. The village of Grange in County Sligo has a Spanish Armada centre that's well worth a visit.

After that came Plantation, when Britain's King James decided to forcibly replace the Gaelic population of Ulster with loyal settlers from England and Scotland. These people resembled the natives to the extent that they left no trace discernible on Irish faces today, although they did leave their mark on Ulster accents. Plantation formed the root of much of the Trouble in Ulster to this day. An interesting examination of Plantation from the perspective of the incoming Scots settlers can be visited at the Monreagh Heritage Centre in East Donegal.

Nowadays, the ease of international travel combined with the opening of the borders of Europe mean that Ireland has experienced an explosion of different cultures and genetic types. Faces met in the pub can be dark or light, brown or blue eyed, blond or black haired. It's an exciting time for our country, and is sure to leave its mark the same way the other influxes of people have done.

Music, Dance and Storytelling

Irish Music

The music of Ireland is one of the few elements of our culture that is homogenous the length and breadth of our country. From buskers on the Cliffs of Moher to accordion players on the streets of Belfast, you'll hear the same recognizable sound from all of them, and experience the same enjoyment in their company.

The music we think of as traditionally Irish came here with the Celts. They picked up Eastern influences in their travels, and to a discerning ear our native tunes have quite a bit in common with the traditional music of the Arab nations. There is a theory that the harp is an instrument with its roots in Egypt and has its roots in an adaptation of the hunting bow.

The oldest tradition is of listening and learning by ear, and although written music is becoming widespread as a defense against the loss of knowledge, purists won't consider scanned sheets or formal learning in passing on their skills. In my opinion it is this element that breathes life into the sound; when musicians gather together for a "session" they follow each other, taking cues and adding flourishes in the same manner that folk music is performed and enjoyed worldwide.

Figure 22 Keeping it alive... by Anna O'Rourke, courtesy of Flickr

Irish traditional music is an unassuming beast. It flourishes in small local pubs and at family get-togethers, which means that those of us who love to hear it played have more opportunity to do so than if the sound was formalized and created by appointment.

The main traditional instruments are the fiddle, Irish flute, tin whistle, Celtic harp, uilleann pipes and bodhrán. It's difficult to believe that the fiddle is an instrument identical to the classical violin; only the manner of playing it is different. Performers delight in ornamentation and not playing a tune the same way twice, and the atmosphere of the session is at least as important as the notes played in judging whether or not it was a success.

Traditional or Sean Nós (translates as "The Old Tradition") singing is less frequently heard, but when you do hear it you'll feel a shiver along your spine and all the hair on your body will stand on end. It's a style usually sung without accompaniment, where the words are at least as important as the tune and the singer is considered to be less of a performer and more of a conduit for the music.

He or she has a great deal of leeway to wring every possible drop of emotion out of his or her listeners. As with instrumental music ornamentation is a key element of the style, and the songs are never sung the same way twice. Sean Nós singing is much more difficult to happen upon than traditional instrumental sessions, and I'd suggest attending the Fleadh Cheoil simply to hear it done well.

If you wish to hear genuine Irish music the way we enjoy it ourselves, I can recommend either Hughes Bar in Chancery St, Dublin (not the Temple Bar music focused on tourists but the genuine article) or the Crane Bar in Galway. If you're in the south of the country, I can recommend De Barra's Folk Club in Clonakilty, County Cork or Mac Diarmada's in Doolin, County Clare.

It's a fact that unvarnished sessions are more common the further you travel from the cities, and the easiest thing to do is just ask a local person. I can guarantee that they'll point you in the direction of a get together that's more of a session than a formal performance of their art.

Irish Dance

Traditional Irish Dancing is going from strength to strength, both here and in all the countries of the world where Irish people have travelled. Watching dancers twirl and step, it's obvious that the skill grew up hand in glove - or, perhaps, foot in shoe - with our traditional music.

In older times Irish Dance was broken into two distinct styles: step dancing, featuring high kicks and complex footwork but where the body and arms remained almost completely still and céilí dancing, which involved moving around the dance floor and which had a lot more in common with country dancing from other cultures.

Céilí dancing is still a feature of Irish country life today, although it's celebrated in our parish halls and dance rooms more seldom than it was a generation back. These days the steps are often "called" in advance, and the activity involves fewer highly skilled practitioners and a lot more hot and sweaty fun.

Step dancing, on the other hand, has become focused more on competition than on performance for its own sake. You'll see girl after girl, and the very occasional boy, perform technically perfect steps with no joy or flair, and with no concept of the individuality or the personality that is so much a part of the Irish performance tradition. I could say that I blame the Riverdance show for this change, but the trend had begun long before that show burst onto the international stage.

If you want to see true Irish dancing as it should be performed, I recommend Sean Nós dancing. As in the singing the phrase translates as "The Old Tradition", and in this case it is a very good thing. Performers usually dance in their own clothing rather than in stylized costumes, and they show a lot more expression and with a lot more freedom to perform to the full extent of the area available to them, especially in their arms and upper bodies.

A subset of Sean Nós dancing is called Brush or Broom dancing, and it's something I strongly recommend if you want to truly understand our dancing tradition. In this style, a dancer wears hard shoes that he or she uses to emphasize the beat of the music. He or she dances with the use of a brush or broom, incorporating the item into the dance with flicks of the feet and a feeling of fun and gladness that can't help but lift the heart.

I do recommend that you experience our traditional dancing while you're here, but if you do I'd suggest you make sure that it's Sean Nós dancing before you go. If you'd like to give it a try yourself then I can suggest the Irish Dancing Workshop in Galway City. Its proprietor, Emma O'Sullivan, is herself a respected dancer and she'll have you jigging and dancing with brushes in less time than you can imagine.

Seanchaí Storytelling

Reading and writing came late to the people of Ireland. We've always loved our stories, though, so the traditional Seanchaí, or combination historian and storyteller, was a well respected person in the community.

In olden times, the storyteller not only retained legends and stories intact from one generation to the next but also kept track of the laws handed down in the epic poems of the people. Nowadays, of course, the role isn't quite so crucial, but the art and passion of the story is burned deep in our psyche.

If you wish to hear a real Irish Seanchaí entertain you, The Brazen Head Bar in Lower Bridge Street, County Dublin organizes a night of dinner and folk-tales where you can enjoy good food and at the same time listen to real Irish stories told in the way they have been for hundreds of years.

Another option is to take part in a storytelling bus tour, where your sights are illuminated and expanded by a storyteller trained in the Seanchaí tradition. The bus is specially designed to provide a true cottage bar experience, and the performance certainly provides a new perspective on the streets of Dublin.

Although the tradition is dying out with the proliferation of TV, podcasts and YouTube, we still have plenty of experienced and enthusiastic practitioners of the art who will be delighted by the opportunity to entertain you.

Irish food and drink

Given that we are a mere handful of generations on from a famine that decimated our population and reshaped our national identity, it should come as no surprise that we Irish people focus hard on our food and drink.

We like to eat well, drink well and we love to share the fruits of our labors. Although these days many of our staple meals are recognizable by people from across the globe - spaghetti Bolognese, lasagna and pizza are particular favorites - thank you, Italy - our old fashioned meals still form a big part of the food our children grow up eating.

Figure 24 Irish Stew and Guinness by daspunkt, courtesy of Flickr

Irish Stew

One of our best known and best loved dishes is Irish Stew. Traditionally this stew was made with mutton, but nowadays beef is standard and some penny-pinching souls even use minced beef. Everybody's mother, Granda and second cousin has their own twist on it, and friendly rivalries break out over whether the gravy should be thick or thin (thick!), or whether it should include parsnips or not (it should, but only the tiniest amount).

What isn't disputed is that the stew should be served with home-made soda bread and that Irish Stew is the perfect meal to serve on a wet winter evening.

Guinness Stout

Another product so closely entwined with Ireland that it can't be disentangled is Guinness stout. It may shock the non-local to know that Guinness is a brand name. Stout is also produced by companies like Murphy's and Beamish and are hotly championed by their patrons, who consider them to be vastly superior to Guinness.

Naturally, the only way to decide fairly is to try all three.

The Guinness storehouse in St. James' Gate, Dublin City offers a tour that explores everything to do with the iconic pint from the fermentation process to the manufacture of the perfect barrel. The tour also comes with a free pint of Guinness at its finish so that you can properly appreciate what you've learned. Only fair, really.

By contrast, Murphy's brewery is located in Cork City, which should explain a great deal about its patrons' passion and their strong and oft expressed hatred of Guinness. The brewery doesn't offer tours, but the Beamish and Crawford does and it's also located in Cork City.

If you want to provoke a passionate debate in any pub in the south of the country, all you need to do is suggest that Guinness makes a better stout than either Beamish or Murphy's. Then lean back and watch the fireworks.

Dillisk / Dulse

Another old-time staple of the Irish diet, and one that is becoming more common as more and more people understand the concept of healthy living, is seaweed. The most commonly enjoyed type is called either Dillisk or Dulse depending on where the speaker grew up and is quite simply made up of dried strands of Palmaria palmata seaweed.

Dillisk has a delicious saltiness and a distinctive nutty flavor. It's rich in iron, iodine and B12, Magnesium and Zinc just to name a few elements and has been used for generations to treat the thyroid problems that so frequently crop up in Irish people.

Aside from that dillisk is a delicious and healthy snack that can be enjoyed without guilt.

Another seaweed regularly consumed here is Carrageen Moss. Given the name you could be excused for expecting it to be green and furry, but in fact the seaweed is a dark red color and bears a surface resemblance to dillisk, so much so that one of its traditional names is "máthair an duilisc" or mother of dillisk.

Although Carrageen Moss has also been widely consumed for decades if not centuries, unlike dillisk it is not enjoyed as a snack in its natural state but is instead used as a thickening agent in jellies, puddings and soups.

Cheese

We Irish love our cheese, and not only that but we're very talented at making it.

The Irish artisan dairy industry is barely thirty years old, but in that time it has expanded to include a range of farmhouse cheeses from almost fifty distinct manufacturers. The growth of cheese-making in this country as an artisan item rather than as a mass-produced item repeats the key themes of enthusiasm and individuality, which by now you know are central to everything we do here.

The majority of our cheeses are vegetarian, i.e. produced without rennet, and they range from tart goats' cheeses to tangy blues and smooth hard yellows. Among my particular favorites are the semi-soft Ardrahan with its lactic saltiness and the very fine and sweet-flavored Triskel with its line of ash along the centre.

I'm quite sure that your preferences will vary from mine, and the wonderful thing is that there are so many fine Irish cheeses available that it's a quest all its own to find and sample all of them.

Coddle

Coddle is a dish that the Dublin cohort rhapsodize about, although those of us in the rest of the country aren't all the way convinces. It had its beginnings in the need to use leftovers, so it comes with no formal recipe or list of ingredients.

In its most common form coddle involves boiling bacon and sausages in a good quality stock then adding potatoes, onions and other vegetables arranged in layers. It might sound simple but its nourishing and ideal for those dull, wet autumn evenings we seem to see so much of.

Try it and let your Dublin friends know what you think of it. You might even make up the ground you lost during the Guinness versus Beamish fiasco.

FOR ME IT WOULD BE THE CRYBEENS THAT WOULD BE YUCK!

Barmbrack

You'll notice that the foods featured here tend to be predominantly savory in flavor. The reason for this is that we have many more recipes for dinners than we do for sweets, likely a holdover from our post-Famine days when we focused intensely on producing enough good food for our families to eat.

An exception to this is the báirín breac or speckled bread traditionally eaten at Halloween. The barmbrack is slightly sweet but not as much so as a cake, and is often buttered before it is eaten. The tradition of the barmbrack isn't so much in its taste as in what's inside it.

Traditionally, barmbrack contains charms like a gold ring, a stick, a piece of rag and a coin. Each charm is carefully wrapped before it's added, and ideally each person who partakes will receive a charm in his or her slice to predict the fortunes of the year to come. Meanings are self-explanatory, with the ring signifying marriage, the coin wealth, the rag poverty and the stick advising that the unlucky recipient would be beaten by his or her spouse!

Many of our Halloween traditions have given way to US-type trick-or-treating, but I'm happy to say that the barmbrack is still going strong. Watch out for it if you happen to visit from mid-October.

Colcannon

Another Halloween staple, though one that hasn't survived as strongly as barmbrack, is colcannon. In its simplest form the dish consists of fried cabbage mixed through mashed potato and seasoned with butter, salt and pepper.

Similarly to the barmbrack, on Halloween a number of charms are wrapped in clean paper twists and added to the colcannon mixture. Ideally each diner will receive one charm in his or her portion, and that charm would predict what would come in the year ahead.

I'm sure I'm not alone in thinking that a warm, buttery slice of barmbrack is preferable to a bowlful of potatoes and cabbage, no matter what charm either one might hold.

Boxty or Potato Bread

With our national dependence on the potato it isn't surprising that a potato-based recipe would feature high on our list of distinctive Irish foods.

The name boxty is an Anglicization of the original name of "arán bocht tí" or poorhouse bread. It's made of a combination of boiled mashed and finely-grated raw potato combined with flour, salt and a tiny amount of milk, and then it's fried in the pan and eaten while it's hot.

Regional variations include all-raw or all-cooked potato, the use of buttermilk or egg and the inclusion of finely diced onion into the mix. I can confirm that all are wonderful and that there is no food on this earth like boxty when recovering from the overindulgence of the night before.

Crubeens

One final Irish food included for old times' sake is Crubeens. Again, this is an Anglicization of the original name of cruibín or pig's trotters. I'm sure you don't need any further help in figuring out what the dish is.

Crubeens are traditionally boiled, then battered, fried and eaten by hand. They went through a decades-long slump when affluence levels reached a peak that meant very few people were compelled to eat the subsistence foods of their parents and grandparents.

Crubeens are currently making a comeback in fine dining circles, a prime example of the old traditional foods being given a new and modern twist. Watch out for them when you're eating out in Dublin or Cork, and feel free to make your own choice about whether to explore this old taste made new.

Chapter 11: A Warm Irish Welcome

Figure 25 Bicycle by Nevin Price-Meader, courtesy of Flickr

Having borne with me throughout my long ramble about life in Ireland both ancient and modern, it won't come as a surprise to learn that our key national attributes are good nature, a passionate support of what we think is right and a strong propensity to have fun.

We have our cultural backbone and our love of literature and the arts, but we don't take ourselves too seriously and the elements we look for are participation and joy.

Whether your passion is fishing or architecture or the fiddle, you'll find like-minded souls here who will be happy to involve you in their pleasure. So plan your trip, pick your destination and look around to see what's on offer there. I promise there'll be plenty.

Fáilte romhat.

PS: Can I Ask You For A Special Favor?

Hopefully this guidebook has given you some ideas about what to do during your stay in Ireland!!

We would like to ask you for a favor, would you be kind enough to leave a review for this book on Amazon? It'd be greatly appreciated!

Thanks a lot.

Preview of "Vienna - By Locals"

We edit and publish travel guides from several cities in the world, all written by locals. When you plan your next destiny, please check on Amazon if we are covering that city already. If not, we will probably writing about it soon, please give us some time.

We would like to give you an advance of our Vienna Guide, which is very special. Please take a look:

Chapter 1: Preface - Vienna By A Local

This book can be used as a complete and unique travel guide for those who are planning on traveling to Vienna. After a short introduction into the topic, the reader will find the first chapter as being dedicated to the top reasons why anyone would want to travel to Vienna. Among these reasons, you will find the Spanish Riding School, the Vienna Philharmonic, the famous Viennese Schnitzel, Austrian wine taverns and the imposing Stephansdom. The second chapter contains the best travel tips from Vienna locals, with reference to the best coffee shops, the different neighborhoods and the Viennese outskirts. You can also find useful information on choosing a bar or a club in Vienna, on the Wi-Fi quality in this European capital and on unique places that only locals know about.

The third chapter is quite interesting, as it is dedicated to those who are interested in traveling to Vienna on a budget. Here, you will find important tips on the things that are free in Vienna, allowing you to save important sums of money. You will also have the opportunity to read specific details on the Vienna tourist card, which offers discounted prices to different tourist attractions and free transportation. In this chapter, you can read about the cheap accommodation opportunities that are available in Vienna.

Vienna travel basics, such as those related to the documents you may need, are presented in the fourth chapter. You will also be offered information about the time differences between Vienna and other locations, about the best time to visit Vienna and about the necessity to make reservations in advance for certain concerts or shows. When reading this chapter, you will know that you are prepared for your future trip to

Vienna. You can then continue reading the fifth chapter, in which you will discover everything there is to know about the public transportation system in Vienna. Here, you will be presented with the different transportation choices you have available, such as the tram, bus or underground line. We tell you information about tickets, their price and how they can be validated.

The sixth chapter provides a brief review over the best restaurants and hotels in Vienna. You will have the opportunity to discover ten of the finest hotels in the city, each with some short information. The second part of the chapter is dedicated to the ten best restaurants of Vienna, each with its individual cuisine and qualities. The seventh chapter concentrated on the numerous cultural opportunities that you will discover during your stay, while the eighth chapter is rather addressed to the shopping opportunities that are available in Vienna. The book ends not with a conclusion but rather with a beautiful portray of Vienna, with valuable information being found in-between the lines.

This book is a wonderful read and it is filled with a wealth of useful information, so do not hesitate to recommend it to anyone who is planning on traveling to Vienna in the near or distant future.

Chapter 2: Top Reasons Why You Should Visit Vienna

In Vienna, everywhere you turn, you feel like you're in another world. There is something in the air, a strong collective memory of the times that are gone and yet still present. If this is the first time you are visiting Vienna, you need to do all the touristy stuff, no matter how cliché they may sound. One of the reasons to consider Vienna as your destination is the Spanish Riding School (Michaelerplatz 1; tel.: +4315339031; http://www.srs.at). With a tradition extending over a period of 400 years, the Spanish Riding School is one of the finest things to discover in Vienna. If you want to experience even more of the Viennese imperial atmosphere, this is the place for you to be. The Lipizzaner stallions, along with their elegant riders, put on an amazing show. You will find yourself applauding at their impressive skills and obvious dexterity.

For music lovers, Vienna is the ideal destination. Even as you are taking a stroll down the crowded streets, you can hear classical music. On cold winter nights, when it is heavily snowing and there are not many people on the street, you will encounter a guy with a wig and Mozart costume trying to sell you tickets for classical music concerts. These concerts are especially arranged for tourists but if you really want to see something special, you have to buy a ticket for the Vienna Philharmonic (Kärnter Ring 12; tel.: +4315056525; http://www.wienerphilharmoniker.at/). This is, without any doubt, one of the most amazing orchestras of classical music in the world. A special treat is also represented by the Vienna Boys' Choir (tel.: +4312163942; http://www.wienersaengerknaben.at/_1), singing for mass every Sunday morning.

Food is definitely a strong reason why you would want to visit Vienna, with the famous Viennese schnitzel standing at the top of the list. This is a little insider tip I am giving to you: the most delicious and gigantic Viennese schnitzel you can eat at Figlmueller (Wollzeile 5; tel.: +4315126177; http://www.figlmueller.at/en/). Another traditional dish that you have to try out is the

Tafelspitz, which is made with boiled beef and horseradish. As a local, I can recommend Plachutta (Wollzeile, 38; tel.: +4315121577; http://www.plachutta.at/de/home/) as the best place to visit if you want to try out the above-mentioned dish. Vienna also has an amazing tradition when it comes to desserts; there is nothing else so sweet and utterly delicious as the Viennese strudel, purchased from any of the small patisseries. However, if you want a dessert that is almost decadently sweet, you have to try out the Sacher Torte. This amazing dessert is made completely from chocolate, with apricot jam in between the layers. A rich chocolate cream covers the delicious Sacher Torte and once you taste it, you will never find another dessert that is sweet as this one.

You cannot come to Vienna, taste its ambrosial food and not savor a perfectly good glass of wine. In the past few years, Austrian wine has started to become more and more popular among wine enthusiasts. Even if you are not a fan of wine, you have to visit a wine tavern, at least once. These wine taverns are normally located in the outskirts of Vienna, many of them being part of the vineyard where the wine is actually produced. Imagine yourself enjoying a delicious meal, with a well-matched glass of wine and feeling more relaxed than you have ever felt in your life. Recommendations of wine taverns in Vienna include the renowned Heuriger Wieninger (Stammersdorfer Straße 78; tel.: +4312924106; http://www.heuriger-wieninger.at/) and Weinbau Gobel (Stammersdorfer Kellergasse 131; tel.: +436642439835; http://www.weinbaugoebel.at/#_=_).

Most of the European capitals have impressive buildings, with churches being often included in the top reasons why you should visit a particular city. When you come to Vienna, you need to check out Stephansdom (Stephansplatz 3; tel.: +431515523054; http://www.stephanskirche.at). This is not your ordinary church and it you will certainly leave you speechless. Don't waste your time trying to appreciate its style but rather take it all in. Clear your mind of other thoughts and try to think about its size and what an amazing presence you have in front of your eyes. There are not many buildings in the world that deliver such feelings; step inside the dome and allow yourself to remain without words. Feed yourself with its uniquely intricate details; if you are in luck, you can visit the dome during a sermon. This is lucky before you will have the opportunity to listen to the choir and the amazing pipe organ.

If you are an architecture enthusiast, Vienna is the right place to visit. You do not even have to go very far, in order to discover its fantastic architecture. Take a stroll down the Ringstrasse, the famous boulevard that was made in 1857, as the command of Emperor Franz Josef I. Not only you will feel like an ant passing by these imposing buildings but, if you know a thing or two about architecture, you will remain without words at the diversity of architectural styles contained in such a short distance. There is the town hall (Friedrich-Schmidt-Platz 1; tel.: +43152550; http://www.wien.gv.at/verwaltung/rathaus/) which is a beautiful display of Flemish and Gothic styles, the buildings of the Vienna University (Universitätsring 1; tel.:+43142770; http://www.univie.ac.at/) belong to the Renaissance style, the famous Burgtheater (Universitätsring 2; tel.: +431514444140; http://www.burgtheater.at) is built in the neo-baroque style and the Parliament (Dr.-Karl-Renner-Ring 3; tel.:

+431401100; http://www.parlament.gv.at/) is part of the neo-classical Viennese architecture. Could you honestly wish for something more?

The Danube is certainly one of the most beautiful things to discover in Vienna but there are not many people that know about the Donauinsel. This is actually a small island in the middle of the Danube River but it has numerous opportunities for relaxation and entertainment. Apart from the relaxing strolls that you can take through the winding alleys, you can enjoy yourself with a group of friends at one of the modern bars or fancy restaurants. If you are the active type, who enjoys the open outdoors, you can go canoeing, bicycling or rollerblading. There is even a beach and you can go swimming in the Danube.

Speaking about entertainment, a great reason to visit Vienna is Prater (Prater 9; tel.: +4317280516; http://www.prater.at/). This amusement park has everything you and your family could ever want. There are mini-golf courses for those with a less reduced passion for adrenaline, colored carousel rides for small kids and scary, yet fun amusements to discover, such as the Hall of Mirrors of the Ghost Train. Here, you will have the opportunity to discover the big wheel that has become one of Vienna's symbols. Also, if you love water parks, there is a special section dedicated to such kind of entertainment.

These are just a couple of reasons why anyone would want to visit Vienna. However, as soon as you visit this city, you will come up with even more on your own.

policies, processes, or directions contained within is the solitary and utter responsibility of the recipient reader. Under no circumstances will any legal responsibility or blame be held against the publisher for any reparation, damages, or monetary loss due to the information herein, either directly or indirectly.

Respective authors own all copyrights not held by the publisher.

The information herein is offered for informational purposes solely, and is universal as so. The presentation of the information is without contract or any type of guarantee assurance.

The trademarks that are used are without any consent, and the publication of the trademark is without permission or backing by the trademark owner. All trademarks and brands within this book are for clarifying purposes only and are the owned by the owners themselves, not affiliated with this document.